Humanity's Fate

By

Peter Bell

© Copyright 2021 by Peter Bell – All rights reserved.

It is not legal to reproduce, duplicate, or transmit any part of this document in either electronic means or printed format. Recording of this publication is strictly prohibited.

Dedication

To Joe Kennedy, the Genius, John's father!

Before the 1929 crash, he was rich. Afterward he became powerful because he saw it coming!

Table of Content

About the Author ii

Introduction 1

These Forces Work Against Us 3

      The Monster Is Among Us 7

Argentina's Bankruptcy 9

The Titanic Takes a Vacation 11

The Virus Just Wanted to Restore Balance to The Planet 14

Who Will Decide Our Future? 16

      Why Have Governments Funded Everything? 17

      Do We Have Options, Possible Solutions to Get Out of This? 20

Is The Credit Going to End? 21

Where Is the Hope? 24

      Optimize The Future as Quickly as Possible 26

We Are Looking for an Idol, A Prophet! 29

      The Solution of the Lesser Evil 30

We Occupy the Minds with The Various Facts 33

Are We Talking About Science Fiction or A Bad Nightmare? ...35

      This Is How the Economy of a Country Works 37

January 20, 1961 39

An Education to Redo 41

The Police State Replaces the Welfare State 44

Final Warning 48

Reality Scares Us 48

Introduction

Yes, there is really an Emergency. The urgency to act because everything could change in three or four years. Suppose we're lucky, just seven or eight years from now.

Is it too late to act?

Can we still avoid the worst consequences of our choices?

Good questions!

Today is October 18, 2021.

No, I am not announcing the end of the world to you. Instead, <u>I am announcing the end of A World that will never be like the one we have all known in the past.</u>

There was 9/11. Okay, but here we're talking about something much more serious, much deeper. These are upheavals that will affect us all for a very long time to come. Upheavals; which will change the entire structure of the Company and consequently our lifestyles.

When we are young, we play in lace. When we were young, we played in lace in a world that was going relatively well. Today even our young people are not really having fun. They are obsessed with their future. A Future they would like to be better, **something that would look a bit like our past, what we (the lucky ones) went through!**

Fortunately, some people can **see clearly**. Those who know that our time looks too much like the end of an Empire. Like that of the end of the Roman Empire, a kind of world where everything seems to go wrong around us. Some kind of bizarre future where ignorance praises disinformation. We will also look at this Phenomenon in the following pages.

The civilization of leisure?

Forget it! This is the old story. Know, understand, control, but why? To try to get through as best as possible? But through what?

I advise you to take a deep breath.

These Forces Work Against Us

Philosophy is a complex world. For the first time in my life, I realized that **macroeconomics** was thousand times more so.

In March 2020, when Italy and France were grappling with COVID-19 for a few days at the start of the crisis, I realized that I no longer understood anything.

For the first time in my life, the perception of a problem required real reflection. It was a big, huge problem!

I thought about it for a few days. I could already see the Tempest advancing. And then, quickly, I grasped the gravity of the situation.

But immediately, I saw that I was wasting my time. I told someone I knew about it—a multimillionaire at the head of a media empire. He did not understand the gravity of the situation.

I wrote to him that I wanted him to publish in one of his major dailies.

The following text was written on **March 16, 2020.**

Coronavirus:

Too late to react?

When the solution makes us sicker than the problem!

We already know a lot about the Virus. We now know what to do to protect ourselves: **Mask and distancing, hand washing, and no regrouping!**

We also know who he attacks. We also know how many are attacked and the percentage of the total number who lose the fight.

We don't have a vaccine, but now we know how to slow it down and fight it.

What to do now?

Are we going to continue to shut it down and fund everything for six months?

Will we create an economic problem again?

Worse than this Virus? An economic bankruptcy that will we and our children have to pay for the next 30 years?

We are well on our way to creating this MONSTER that will be a hundred times worse than accepting this disease.

A pandemic?

What is a pandemic?

A disease that kills more or less 1.5% of only those who catch it?

When a government goes into debt ...

What will happen to you in 6 months, five years, or the next ten years?

What will happen soon will a florist who loses $ 35,000 reopen?

Will, a restaurateur who lost $ 90,000 start over?

NO! There are already thousands of traders who have shut down for good.

Is it too late to act?

Maybe yes, but now is the time to act if the worst is to be avoided. Avoid something a thousand times worse than this Virus: a Depression that could last 10 or 15 years!

Yes, we have to reopen everything tomorrow!

Open everything up, and keep our sanitary measures. It's here only solution to keep our lifestyle.

Inhuman to do so?

In 6 months, it will be too late to start all over again. Debt will kill us and kill any stimulus. Debt will wipe out the middle class.

We will go back to the 1950s when only a privileged few went on vacation to Florida. We're going back to a car for two families.

Who thinks about the future of our children?

Currently, no one. No one sees clearly, and no one is ready to see the reality and act.

Tomorrow!

Forget your pension funds. They might earn you 75% of their current value. Teachers, firefighters, police, and others will lose a lot. They think they are safe!

Accepting reality is accepting to do the right thing right away.

I hope you have thought about it a bit.

I wrote the above text on **March 16, 2020**.

By then, I had already realized that this text was going against the **REASON OF STATE,** but naively I thought that the businessmen would all stand up. They could get up. I thought they understood that we were shaking the foundations of our Company.

It was the only chance we had to get out of it without too much damage. Yet, they did nothing. They fell silent. Too late! Now you have to pay! It's going to hurt to a point where everything is going to change in our lives.

The Monster Is Among Us

Imagine for a second that in 2017 Delta Airlines would have decided to ground its planes and that it would have been the only company to do so. Six months after this hypothetical decision, all his creditors would have put him in bankruptcy. Today, after eighteen months of this medicine, no one is talking about bankruptcy.

What happened to Air France, Delta, Air Canada, and KLM all suffered the same fate. Billions lost with no apparent real and **immediate** consequences.

MSC, Costa, Norwegian Carnival, and all the rest have seen even worse. No bankruptcy. It costs over a billion dollars to build one of those big ships that are 75% funded and ... no consequences at this time.

The same goes for the world of shows, cinema, conferences, catering, and hotels. Unbelievable!

The same goes for the world of Tours operators, cafes, gyms, ... the list goes on and on. Worse yet, some people think that the money they receive is due and will cost them nothing.

Obviously, with such subsidies, some took advantage: the renovators, furniture sellers, Ikeas of this world, etc.

Nothing is like it used to be. Nothing holds. The world we have known only exists for a very long time. Few realize it, and very few understand it. But, very soon, we are all going to experience it.

Argentina's Bankruptcy

I went to Argentina in November 2007, six years after the country's bankruptcy on December 1, 2001.

What happened in Argentina after this bankruptcy? For a while, each province printed its own money, its banknotes. The big banks had fled like thieves. They had abandoned the country and the savers.

I spoke to a lawyer who had $ 250,000 in his account. He lost everything. Before the crisis, the Argentine peso was at par with the US dollar. Six years later, it was only worth 50%.

Who lost?

Retirees have all lost their cash. Those who had debts lost everything.

Who won?

Only those who had gold or real estate without a mortgage. The other CAPUT!

How did Argentina fare?

Quite easily. Since the Western world was not bankrupt, all Argentinian products were real bargains.

Several foreigners bought vineyards, farms, factories… and finally, everything started again. The prices had fallen, and everything started again.

When I was there, Chileans used to go there on vacation. Previously it was the Argentines who went to Val Paraiso in Chile.

Except currently, **with the global economic crisis we are experiencing, who will come and save us?** Anybody! All the countries are on the verge of bankruptcy, very large companies are in technical bankruptcy, and the banks, the key to the solution (the world of finance), will have to make difficult decisions.

The Titanic Takes a Vacation

What happened on April 15, 1912? What really happened?

The boat was sinking. We had to make decisions, and we had to make the right ones. **We took them.** Like the Titanic, our economy is sinking. We had to make the right decisions. Did we take them?

On the Titanic, we chose to save women (mothers) and children first. We saved the future. We, in the face of the COVID, what have we done?

We chose first to save the very old and the very old sick. We saved the past. **We chose to save them at all costs**. The average age of those who died was 84 years old. With the new variants, this average is lowered slightly by the youngest hyper-obese, diabetic, and asthmatics. We made our choices too late.

THE DEBTS ARE THERE.

On the other hand, to save them, everything had to be stopped. Stop everything, even if we already knew that a tiny 0.0001% of the youngest were affected, even that 50% of the population was asymptomatic.

In March 2020, children, young people, and older adults were asymptomatic at the start of this crisis. Before the onset of the Delta variant, 98.99% of people affected were very old and very sick. We have done everything, EVERYTHING for them. We took our time, and instead of getting through it quickly, we allowed the delta variant to come in and spread instead of letting it go naturally.

Gentlemen and ladies' politicians, you all bear the responsibility. You have listened to your epidemiologists, given them the keys to governance, and now we can see where it is leading us all. Plus, I would add that we haven't seen anything yet! It is just beginning.

Well, I'm telling you the following: it's exactly like taking lawyers to build a bridge when you let doctors rule a society. **He's going to collapse soon.**

Firmly in your little university bubble, you thought yourself thinner than a virus. You thought you'd stop him, control him. On the contrary, you allowed the variants to hatch by delaying it, and now that it gets serious, we have no more money. We are CAPUT!

Dear specialists, did you not know anything about the world of viruses?

Be careful; if this Virus had mainly killed children, young people under 20, young adults, and people under 65 in the majority, everything I told you would not hold up.

Did you want to corner me? Well, this corner is yours. Common sense is taking over, and your beautiful theories are starting to fall apart one after the other.

Sweden is pretty much one of the few countries that have reacted well. It was the same Virus, though. They allowed distancing in shops, wore masks, and strongly supported the vaccine without destroying their economy too much.

Why have you never dared to change course? Did you want to show us that you were never wrong? COVID is not Ebola. We were lucky, and now we totally screwed up that luck.

The Virus Just Wanted to Restore Balance to The Planet

This, most did not understand. On the other hand, you will still have to live economically from the consequences of your decisions for much longer than for simple flu. And it's started.

What is a virus?

A virus is a nature that speaks out to defend itself, to progress, to improve. Obviously, for you, this definition is unacceptable. It goes against the very essence of your medical profession. Yet you cannot win. You never can.

What is the role of viruses?

Viruses are obligate parasites of living cells. They can only develop with the forced collaboration of their host. Would they also be regulators of populations? Does this subject scare you?

In the aquatic environment, you have no problem accepting this fact. In humans, you lose your Latin!

When we want to save everything, we lose everything.

So now let's talk about the only thing we have left: the future.

Throughout this saga, we have abandoned the young and old. We let down the under 65s and asked them to sacrifice themselves.

Where is our current society going?

Pretty much no one knows. No one dares to talk about it. It's practically a taboo subject besides being a Reason for State, read: something unassailable.

On the other hand, if we want to get by and prosper and live well, we will have to make the right choices.

Who Will Decide Our Future?

Governments?

Come on; they are hardly used anymore. Worse, they are making the economic crisis worse with every step they take.

Either way, they no longer have any real power. They are all in debt and can hardly do anything. They no longer have a margin. The only thing they have left is to tax us more and more. We take away our freedom subtly by giving ourselves beautiful false moral reasons for doing so.

Cut in their expenses? Rationalize their methods? They are incapable of it. They are not from the private sector. They don't know anything; worse, they have no courage **and try again and again to win votes by wanting to save everyone by increasing the free services… which we all have to pay for.**

Much like the parent who overprotects their child, they make the worst mistake.

On the other hand, their only BIG boss, **the world of Finance**, will soon bar their door. It will be a big blow. The Virus could not do its job; depression and even wars spawned by these phenomena will finish the job.

Natural laws are stronger than anything. To ignore them is to want to hurt yourself even more without ever having understood a thing.

At first, there will be a slight increase in interest rates. Many irresponsible consumers behave like governments, except they do not have the power to tax. Many will leave their skin there. Their creditors aren't going to kill them; no, they're just going to let them vegetate.

Governments always like to postpone important decisions to the Greek calendars, except that today we have arrived at the Greek calendars. There is no other way out.

Why Have Governments Funded Everything?

Not for the same reasons they have in the past. In the past, governments financed infrastructure to improve the productivity of the country. They were funding to help enrich us all.

Today it is the opposite! In doing so, they impoverish us. We can feel it. <u>The billions added to the national debt serve only to avoid social unrest caused by poverty.</u>

Redoing a bridge or a road brings nothing to collective wealth. The delivery truck won't go any faster. Productivity takes its toll on your cold. We put money in our pockets in the short term by giving jobs for no real reason. In doing so, we simply postpone the approaching depression.

Obviously, governments could still tax more. Be careful, and they won't. The borrowing rates are so low that they are taking advantage of the current moment. Even ahead of state went about it with the following sheer imbecility. He said, "Now is a good time to borrow!" ... As if these rates are always going to stay so low!

Our current societies are lagging behind developing countries. These countries have not increased their deficits and will become even more productive in the face of us. We will continue to have almost everything produced by them. Worse, we will be totally dependent on it.

Obviously, the middle class will disappear. It is disappearing faster and faster every year. Governments do not have the courage to say where we are really at. Every day they try to convince us of the opposite. On TV, we are now shown those who are starving to try to cheer us up.

We Are Also Stunned

We are told about pollution and global warming. We are given causes to make us forget the REAL problem: **the economy.**

Politically, it is no longer useful to play green when you are in the red. Yellow looks better on us!

But when will these governments end up admitting that by having wanted to save everyone from clearing their conscience, they have impoverished us all?

Each must rule his Destiny. Sorry but this is the only viable long-term solution. You have to put the crutches aside.

Do We Have Options, Possible Solutions to Get Out of This?

What exactly is the 'lesser evil' solution for treating a patient with cancer?

Do we have cancer that is eating us away, or is it just a coughing fit?

Societal and commercial hyper-credit exploded with the Marshall Plan for post-war Europe. Now, this same excess of credit is slaughtering our throats.

On the other hand, the practice of easy credit for all dates back to the last fifty years. We, individuals, go through this practice. We do not have a choice. If we don't pay, we lose our goods: car, property, etc.

Governments are playing on other fronts. They don't seem to have any limits. Their power to tax is total, and it is always increasing.

Where are we at?

Is The Credit Going to End?

We have seen small countries go bankrupt. A technical bankruptcy. The others survived them. Central banks have immense powers. Unlimited powers?

Can they continue to dictate everything as they see fit? Not for very long!

There will be winners and losers. Who will they be?

<u>The winners will be the least indebted countries</u> because their citizens will be the least taxed. In the past, these countries were lagging. Finished, they will be brought back to the foreground.

Russia has almost no debt. Italy and Portugal are drowning in debt. Chile and Peru have very little debt.

Who will be the losers?

It will be the citizens. We! Here are some concrete examples of winners and losers.

Purgatory could last several years. Why? Simply because today, we do not yet accept the urgency given to us by these data. We continue to promise people and seas to win votes.

Ridiculous! Worse yet, citizens think they deserve this money that it is due to them.

What should we do quickly?

Apply for horse medicine? Especially not. You have to be subtle to avoid revolts and revolutions. Gradually, people will have to adjust, that is, lose their dreams.

We will go from the big car to the small one. From the little one, we will go towards the bike. It will be easy; it will feel like we are saving the planet. Travel: less and less often and closer and closer to home.

Wines? The cheapest. The same goes for cafes and restaurants. **A beautiful new life is full of small pleasures.** We could even dare to call this recipe: **voluntary simplicity.**

We will treat those who travel by plane as polluters. We will want electric cars and forget the five nuclear power plants that had to be built to power them.

We will never say that there are too many people on the planet. We will call these planners killers, racists. We will no longer understand anything, and we will accuse those who have succeeded in life as the worst polluters responsible for all our ills.

Finally, there will be the Elite and the Others. No more in-between, the middle class. With artificial intelligence, we need fewer hands. Arms, yes, we need them, but a lot less than before. We just invented the machine that collects broccoli. Yes, and not all of the broccoli! Only that of a size determined according to customer needs. The machine will return later to the same field for the others.

The contribution of artificial intelligence will be endless. It will lower production costs and help bring jobs closer to home. A real double-edged sword, but at least good news.

Obviously, this will not be the end of everything—only a good part. Humans, in general, understand absolutely nothing until it hurts enough. They will only quit smoking on the advice of their doctors, not before. They will change their diet after their heart attack, not before.

His emotions outweigh his sanity 95% of the time. We only condemn when we can't take it anymore. This goes for everything: politics, food, love, etc.

A tiny minority is saved by their intelligence. Instead of taking pills, they change their diet. They listen to their body, mind, and their reasons.

They react in time.

Where Is the Hope?

In the memory. In memory and the will.

Passions, phobias, nothing will make us a slave anymore. We will 'do the best.'

The exception does not prove the rule. We ignore the rule. Why?

This is how. Repeat the same mistakes. Whoever ignores the lessons of history are doomed to repeat them. Yes, except for those who will have the courage.

We learn from our mistakes. Truly? Make me laugh.

One-day murderer, always a murderer. Yes, the second time is too many.

What to do then?

Accept and recognize. This is the first step towards recovery.

Accept and recognize that we are no longer the best. Recognize that they have surpassed us on several points these countries that were described **as developing**.

And above all, live within our means. Stop borrowing. Yes, our standard of living is going to take some for his cold. Normal, you have to pay this credit card once and for all.

Yes, we have dominated the world. Now we share it. Difficult to understand, see or accept?

Thirty years ago, it was the other way around. They weren't coming to visit us from the South of Asia. Now, this is it. The transformation was hardly noticeable at first, difficult to grasp. We were getting poorer very slowly. During this time, they were getting rich pretty quickly. You understand?

Are you starting to see it too? It is foreigners who occupy the terraces of our cafes. We are seated behind.

Kind of like spoiled children who never have and have to fight. We didn't even know there was a war. They knew it. They were emerging from poverty. Well done! If at least we had had a little ambition, we wouldn't have let ourselves be passed so easily.

What do we really need?

Shock treatment?

Unfortunately, we are still sinking. We're not ready yet. Today nothing is going well. With fifteen engineers, we can move all automobile production to their countries. Why not? We are lowering the prices after all.

Yes, but at what price?

It is a complex society. Macroeconomics is complex.

Optimize The Future as Quickly as Possible

Necessity is the mother of inventions. Help mom. This need, this urgency to act, we feel it more and more. It is as if the COVID has accelerated history. We've sunk so quickly since the start of 2020. Were we that rich then?

What have we done?

Currently, it is impossible to know if the solution will hurt or very severely. I opt for the second possibility.

The world of tomorrow will be made up of the rich in the USA and the rich in France. It will be made up of the rich from Morocco and the rich from Germany. Wealthy people from Peru, Egypt, Turkey, and Canada. And so on.

There will also be the poor of the USA and France. The poor of Morocco and Germany, etc.

<u>Gone are the middle classes</u>. Inflation and interest rates will kill them. Their debts which represented their false access to wealth, will completely strangle them.

I don't see a solution for them. The state will gradually stop taking care of them because he won't do it anymore. The elderly will have to stay at home and take care of their grandchildren ... like in the 1950s. These years to come, I call them the SACRIFICE YEARS.

It will not be easy to go back, but it will have to be done with.

This scenario is not so great and will only work if there are no surprises like a real pandemic, war, or cataclysm. So there, only the super-rich will still be able to enjoy life. We are made so fragile that the slightest shock can bring down the System.

Unemployment will make a comeback for many. We were off to a good start to hit that wall, but the history of the COVID threw us headfirst very quickly towards this precipice.

In just two years, several governments have doubled their debts past fifty years.

I, therefore, feel the extreme urgency to have this manuscript published before these events take place.

Today, I am a bit of a loner, but everyone will prove me right in four or five years.

So optimizing for the future can only happen if we dare to admit our mistakes and go through the suffering. Otherwise, the scenario will be even darker.

Necessity gives us hope.

Take the city of London in 1750, and everyone was heating with wood. In 1850, it was the turn of coal, and the air was becoming unbreathable. Then there was the oil period, and now we are bathing in much cleaner energies.

Did we need a great scientific demonstration to make us understand these things?

Obviously, no! Everything has followed the normal course of evolution.

A kind of adaptive faculty.

We Are Looking for an Idol, A Prophet!

I hate prophets as I hate hysterics. I hate those who take advantage of the naivety of the good people to fill their pockets—those who fly all the time and pride themselves on being greens.

I hate the profiteers of great causes because these causes carry in themselves the solution to our problems. As with the London example, the choices will come at the right time. High oil prices are the best way to move towards other solution (s).

We never look at the real causes of the problems. Take the case of the Nile, for example. In 1960, the population of Egypt was 26.6 million people. Egypt's population today exceeds 102 million. In 1960 Sudan had a population of 7.5 million people. Today more than 36 million people live there. Other countries also use the Nile for their consumption, industries, and agriculture. Five other countries also take Nile water from Lake Victoria.

Who here questioned **overpopulation** as the sole responsible for this imbalance?

Anybody! It would be immoral! This is the only reason besides the roadblocks! No one is talking about overpopulation.

On the contrary, we praise those who want to save more and more lives with vaccines.

No one is talking about birth control. If the Chinese had not controlled their population, there would be a billion more Chinese to feed. A billion more! For me, it smacks of war! It is irresponsible.

Here, Europe serves as a model for us. In 1960 the population of France was 46.62 million people; today, there are 67.5 million inhabitants in France, only 44% more, while for Egypt, there is talk of an increase of 290%. This is the heart of the matter.

Despite all the advances in agriculture for irrigating land, the planet still has its limits. The Virus is there to control this factor. And because we prevent him from doing his job, we are heading straight for something a thousand times worse: wars and famines.

The Solution of the Lesser Evil

The patient is very ill, and the more clairvoyant see his agony. Is there a possible solution?

It is unthinkable for most people to visualize that, in this world where everything was going relatively well, that 2020 and 2021 have delivered the final blow. It is, however. **We are**

beginning to witness the end of history as we have always known it.

Nothing will be more accessible like before. On the other hand, there is only one solution that remains possible to avoid the worst. This solution assumes that everything remains constant. If a war, a cataclysm or a significant increase in interest rates occurs, then forget about it. Nothing will work anymore. We will then experience another long and deep depression.

And if another virus takes its toll, there will be no possible solution—more money to fight it.

Here is the only possible solution. It is about repaying our mistakes in the best ways sweet possible. Each citizen will have to pay more or less $ 500 more per year in taxes of all kinds for several years to erase this debt. At the same time, governments will have to seriously and **really** cut social measures and lower the wage bill of their employees. Consumption will be reduced, and there will be a slight contraction of the economy and an increase in the unemployment rate. No other alternative is possible. It will bring us social unrest, strikes, suicides, etc. It will be the end of a world as we have known it in the past.

Moreover, if our workers cannot be quickly better than those of the developing countries, forget this solution. We will no longer have any alternative.

Finally, we will have to learn to live in decline, **a bit like retirees.** It is possible to live in a world where the growth of the Gross National Product no longer exists. This decrease could even bring us nice surprises such as a drop in the prices of several everyday items. You just have to live differently.

So, finally, after 20 or 25 years of discipline, there might be the hope of returning to that civilization of leisure that we were promised in the past. I really wish it on our children.

Utopia is part of the solution! You must try!

We Occupy the Minds with The Various Facts

Every newsletter devotes an interesting portion of its time to the news. An animal caught in a trap, a little girl falling into a hole, a vehicle swinging on the ramp of a bridge, etc.

Okay, that's all excellent. Everyone understands it. However, this same bulletin never says that the national debt has increased by $ 30,000,000 today. No one cares. What is the actual proportion of the audience that is truly capable of abstracting?

Too bad because today it is catching up with us. What do we do with that little girl who fell into a well if we can't even fill up on gas?

What do we do with that truck dangling on the ramp of a bridge when we hear about a 15% pay cut. What do we do with this football team that has occupied all of our evenings when we lose our job?

We let OTHERS control our lives. They won. We gave them our vote… and we continue!

There is one thing we cannot erase: GOVERNMENT DEBTS! For thirty years, they were allowed to impoverish us until everything started to crumble. At this point, we took to the street. Too late.

The only solution to get out of this: have plenty of money to keep having fun with the less than 500 dollars in your pocket.

Soon we won't even need cashiers. Everything becomes electronic. What to do for these cashiers? Can they convert to flight attendants? Frankly, I don't know. We have come to the following conclusion: what will happen with most of our work in 10 or 20 years?

We can no longer choose according to the Present. We must now look very far to avoid having part of our lives stolen by technology.

There are too many of us on the planet. Otherwise, it would be Paradise.

Are We Talking About Science Fiction or A Bad Nightmare?

We are not talking about a new reality that will appear to us to have wanted to be responsible. A world that has its natural laws that we don't want to accept.

You raise your child by wanting him to be responsible. We do not apply at all the same rules for the Company.

Alcohol exists for fun. Many use it to destroy themselves. Success lies in measurement. Too many men want a bigger boat than their neighbors. We want a nicer car, a bigger house.

We have transported these abuses throughout society. If no one understands, we will need a Dictatorship. She is getting closer to us. The Dictatorship is born of poverty. We're heading straight for it.

The pendulum of the animal world teaches us that only the strong survive. We are too weak. We refused to respect this law. Now she's catching up with us.

We pride ourselves on not being racists. We are by nature. Animals kill the weak to improve the breed so as not to delay the herd. We help him, and we give him everything.

We do a thousand times worse than animals. We kill those who do not speak our language. We kill those whose skin color is different from ours. We kill those who do not have the same religion as us. When are we going to understand and accept who we really are?

Never, probably never! In addition, people who have never experienced this situation are outraged by these comments. They are not racist but do not hang out with those of another religion or color.

We are paying millions to give people with Alzheimer's disease twelve more months. But what are we doing to help young people get started in business? Those who have a life ahead of them! Not much.

We are working the other way around. Not like on the Titanic, but upside down! The old come before the young. The weak before the strong. The sick, we have done everything for them. Let's face it. We no longer respect natural laws.

We have wasted our heritage. Worse yet, we are no longer discussing. **We no longer question anything. We are afraid,** and we accept everything like sheep.

This Is How the Economy of a Country Works

If we don't understand this question, what good would any discussion be? Here is how it actually works.

Where does a country's economic wealth come from?

Of its exports!

Indeed. Exports bring money from other countries into our own. This is the only key to success. When I buy a pair of socks at the corner store, the business owner takes that money to buy ice cream for his whole family. These internal exchanges do not bring anything back to the country, as such... except a sales tax.

On the other hand, when an Egyptian buys a Boeing, when a Chinese buys a Californian wine, when an Englishman buys an American car, a tractor, or a warplane, we are talking about wealth. When a boat full of wheat is exported, or a computer product is sold worldwide, we talk about wealth.

Only with this money will we determine the salary that we will give to all people paid by the State, both those paid by Municipalities or any other government body. We hear firefighters, police officers, nurses, teachers, civil servants, etc.

This is why American teachers earn much more than Mexican teachers.

Warning! This is exactly how a country works. It doesn't work the other way around.

So what have we been doing for the past two years? **We have crippled the private sector to a level that will greatly affect the public sector ... in addition to ruining state finances.**

Until what point?

This question is easy to answer. The public sector is responsible for the success of the private sector. The coffers are empty, and the citizens are overtaxed.

So there have to be dark days, even years, for all those paid by the state.

Could it be even worse? Yes, and it will be and more.

In the next stock market collapse, pension plans will be greatly affected. In the best of all worlds, I expect retirement premiums to drop from 5% to 15%.

We will have no choice. We will have to do everything to avoid the total collapse of pension systems.

If you recognize this fact, you are on the fast track to understanding the Future. Otherwise, you will simply be taken by surprise, enraged, and without having understood anything.

Good luck!

January 20, 1961...

In his inaugural address, President Kennedy said: 'Don't ask yourself what the country can do for you. Instead, ask yourself what you can do for the Country. "

Imagine a Democratic President who enunciates the same principle today. Just imagine for a few seconds someone who would say: give to the state first! He would be pilloried on the spot.

As we have evolved. Today everything is owed to us. Unbelievable. We have become the center of the planet. Without us, nothing more happens.

During a trip to Cuba in the 1970s, two doctors told me how avant-garde Cuba was: free school, complementary medicine, etc. Each time they answered, I told them: 'We have all of this too.' This get-all mentality has made us dependent on the state. Instead of taking charge, we thought the state should do it.

A beautiful historical era that ends; we will have to rediscover the sense of responsibility. **'To each according to his merit'** will become the new norm. Marx has never been so capitalist. Good luck to the spoiled babies.

An Education to Redo

We are capable of educating our children. Education is something else. To educate implies a system of values to be taught, and to choose it requires judgment and experience. Our early childhood educators hold the reins that will guide our young people in their hands.

Everything starts from this point. If twenty teachers were asked to choose these values , we would probably have twenty different answers.

The disempowerment starts very early. We have disoriented minds. The weak one is always saved by the strong one. Support is already there. Passive, the victim has not to wait for someone to come and rescue her.

Twenty years later, in adulthood, it will always be so. The state must provide me with a job. Where does this philosophy come from?

Who are we to believe that we owe it to ourselves to take care of ourselves?

The initiative is little valued. We are waiting for help. We don't move. Nice picture!

The company has gradually become stiffened over the years. Let's take care of those who can't get on their own. Why?

To give yourself a clear conscience?

The system is ridiculous. We are incapable of accepting Reality. We cover it. We bandaged her. **In doing so, we give ourselves a good conscience.**

And in doing so, we are widening this deficit which is therefore right for us. Except that, for us, it will be too late! We, too, should be taken care of.

Let us take responsibility for our destiny. Let's roll up our sleeves. The real fight will soon begin. The real struggle has always existed in Mexico and all those countries that used to be called **banana republics**, where the state could not afford to take care of its citizens.

Suppose he manages to do it in life by his genius and intelligence: well done! By nature, humans will always seek the easiest path, the one which requires the least effort. On the other hand, we must stop thinking that everyone has a right to it.

Everyone will have to stand up at the same time and say enough is enough. **We will not do this out of courage;** we will do it out of obligation, simply because we no longer have a choice.

Since the start of the COVID era, we have seen the number of dropouts double. At first, this vision was shocking. They are everywhere downtown. Now we got used to it, and seeing their misery values our success even more. It's believed, but it's true. Once again: To each according to his merit. Let us stop widening our deficit only to give us a good conscience <u>and finally want to buy votes.</u>

Healing begins with effort.

The Police State Replaces the Welfare State

To succeed in this cleaning of the mind, it will cost us great efforts. At first, these tumults and popular revolts will have to be broken! We will have to set new standards.

You don't have to be called Nostradamus to predict the future. As with the Little Prince by St-Exupéry, all you have to do is ask the Sun to rise at the first light of day.

Yes, all perspectives will change. Each will become responsible for his destiny. Aid measures will remain, but they will be minimal. On the other hand, scholarships must remain. University is too expensive for those who have talent but lack the money to develop it.

Yes, we must help young people, give them a chance. The old people, on the other hand, have had a lifetime to prove themselves. They don't need us anymore. We are responsible for what we sow. At worst, they will go back and live with their children as they have always been done except for the last fifty years.

Think about it for a second, is it normal to work thirty years and then receive state benefits for forty years? Ridiculous. It is this upside-down world that has ruined us all. This mistake will be remembered for a long time to come.

We can no longer escape on the backs of others. The so-called Rich (in the streets) put in great effort and hired many people for a long time. They deserve all our admiration. Let them be left alone. Without them, millions of workers would have lived in abject poverty.

The socialist countries discouraged these entrepreneurs who went to live elsewhere. Do you want to continue murdering those who have fed you for years?

So keep lying to yourself. Your future will serve as a lesson to you. We used to admire these entrepreneurs. For fifty years, they have been called the exploiters of the people. Shoo them away, and you will no longer have to pay union dues! Well, you do.

The Welfare State will become the Police State because it will protect our gains instead of squandering them for votes.

Whoever pays his debts gets richer. Officials will have to repeat this sentence to enter work. In addition, any politician will be excluded if he has not previously proven himself in the private sector—**likewise, no more power-obsessed thirty-year-olds without any experience.**

Yes, the world has to be remade. Redo in the sense that we will just have to go back to the values of yesteryear. We will consume without mortgaging our future. We will stop 'living beyond our means.'

Impossible to do otherwise. There is no longer a 'B' plan. Purgatory will last for several years. Gone are the endless vacations—no more retirement before age 60. Either way, we'll have to keep working just to 'get there.'

The standard of living in developed countries will be similar to that of developing countries. It might even continue to increase! That of developing countries will not be really affected.

The day the Dow Jones collapses…

… All the stock markets on the planet will collapse.

In 1928, John Kennedy's father saw this crisis coming.

He had sold off his stocks before the collapse. Before, he was rich. Afterward, he became powerful. We were witnessing the end of 'The Roaring Twenties.' We were in trouble until World War II. His son John later became President.

Soon the stock markets will collapse, and they will not go up as they did in late March 2020. This time will be like in 1929. It will last.

During this time of restriction, what will happen to the 'untouchables' pension funds? Any scenario is possible.

The world will start again, yes, but how? This is how I see it. First, several production tools will be repatriated. Good news! On the other hand, the Gross National Product will have a strong contraction. The middle class will become the working class again.

Purgatory will be long and difficult to accept.

And all this shit, why?

Because we crippled our economies because of the COVID virus, if we had just continued to live, there would have been, I grant you, 5% more deaths, 8% GNP contraction for six months, but we would have gotten through it.

By refusing to recognize the forces of natural laws, we will now lose 100 times more. Yes, wars will happen. Yes, the famine will spread to several countries. Yes, individual dysfunction problems will triple, and eventually, the Virus will have overcome the intelligence of our leaders: there will be millions of more deaths in the end.

Well done, great success!

I take my leave and go on a cruise.

Final Warning

Reality Scares Us

After discussing my manuscript with a few people, I realize the following:

The human brain is incapable of living in insecurity. **The human brain is incapable of living without a response.** When we look at the clouds, we naturally try to structure the image. We see faces, angels or mountains. To keep it simple: they make us think of something. We structure, we organize.

So here, how do you structure something you've never seen?

Solution

Most people are too insecure or too afraid of the unexpected to consider it.

We don't play ostrich because we run away from the real answers; we play ostrich to be safe because we don't know better.

This attitude is the one that will paralyze us the most in the face of the difficult decisions that will await us very soon.

This paralysis can bring us straight to our downfall. To accept whatever reality is to choose to face it at all costs.

Sometimes you have to **suffer to heal.**

Change is our worst enemy. He is now with us.

Changing careers, moving, changing friends… we want to avoid all of these things. On the other hand, if it is for our survival**, we will draw on unsuspected strengths.** Yes, we will have to change society because otherwise, it will take us with it as History has shown us too many times.

www.ingramcontent.com/pod-product-compliance
Lightning Source LLC
Chambersburg PA
CBHW050312220526
45465CB00005B/1962